saving face

saving face

poems selected
1976 -1988

Roy Miki

Turnstone Press

Turnstone Press
607-100 Arthur Street
Winnipeg, Manitoba
Canada   R3B 1H3

Turnstone Press gratefully acknowledges the
assistance of the Canada Council and the Manitoba
Arts Council in the publication of this book.

Cover illustration: Linda Ohama

This book was printed and bound in Canada by
Kromar Printing Limited for Turnstone Press.

Second printing September 1991.

Canadian Cataloguing in Publication Data

Miki, Roy Akira, 1942-

   Saving face: poems selected 1976-1988

   ISBN 0-88801-155-5

I. Title

PS8576.I54S3 1991   C811/.54   C91-097078-5
PR9199.3.M565S3 1991

Acknowledgements

Some of these poems appeared in *Inalienable Rice, Rikka, Asianadian, Island, Redress News* and *Fear of Others*.

The poems in "redress" were all initially written in the air, on board flights for work in the redress movement, 1984-1988.

for Slavia

Contents

redress

a pre face

one: an old photo, my pregnant mother with her childhood friend on a wide and empty street, my two brothers and sister, as small children. branded "enemy alien," they have just been shipped to ste agathe, a small french canadian town 25 miles outside of winnipeg, 1000s of miles from the rolling hills of the fraser valley in bc, from the home in haney with its orchards, garden and creek out back. the traces of silence hover around her young figure, born at the mouth of the skeena river, finding herself in this alien sugar beet farm.

two: 4 years old, in the alley the doorway of a wood-working factory — the whir of machines, the shadowy men in sawdust. the flimsy shack, my grandparents, parents, two brothers and sister, transient relatives coming and going, all of us crowded into three small rooms. my mother and father gone before dawn, returning late at night from work in the city — only brief moments between the pressing emptiness of absences. the stray faces of other jcs in make-shift dwellings. in the (later) move to the city they disappear from the daily.

three: 6 or 7, walking down portage in winnipeg, and a voice — "dirty japs," my mother tightens her grip on my hand. what have we done? no anger, "they don't like us because we look japanese, it's only racial prejudice." the words never go beyond the words.

four: telescoped years, unlearning the mother tongue — the hunger for rock & roll in "the down beats," history receding in the mirrorless huddle of canteens and cars. in the wake of assimilation, the ad after bc, the spoken in the bleached record of memory.

five: the move to vancouver, and my father delighted — so
finally to see his beloved coast, the city of his childhood,
then the retraction, the pulling back, the fear for me in
the face of racism. his last memory of place still locked
in time.

six: lost in a tokyo language school, sounds of childhood
japanese popping into my head — grandmother's voice
entering my dreams. "o-baa-chan, o-baa-chan, gakko iko,"
laughable in a class of five, with an american, german,
frenchman, australian, me — all together now, "o-baa-san."

seven: on the island of kyushu, in fukuoka, home of my
grandparents before canada, tracking down family records
in government archives, but no luck — then a chance
evening with a distant cousin who has two photos of my
grandmother. one in ceremonial kimono, just married, and
another in canada with children, the moment (later)
reconstructed in a poem.

eight: working with other sansei jcs on a photo exhibit "a
dream of riches" — the "journeys" to those "legendary"
places, the "ghost" towns of childhood prairie talk:
greenwood, slocan city, new denver, sandon, lemon creek,
popoff, kaslo. words.

nine: coming on the letters of muriel kitagawa, a nisei
mother of four children, who spoke the outrage and
betrayal of uprooting to her brother wes. the daily turn of
events, inert in family trunks and government files. the
editing a bridge — "i had the queerest sensation of living in
some fantastic dream as the train slowly moved out of the
station. all along the tracks, wherever they could, crowds
of nihonjin lined up to wave good-bye . . . ok we move.
but where?"

sansei

tokyo poem

shadows return one & by one   cling
to a single calla lily   (a yellow
pistle set deep   as desire too is
a conch   a white petal   a surface

to pull the bee   into its mysteries

•

some bamboo poles   strung together
to shield daikon gobo   & lotus roots
the women who pause   to finger them
babies on their backs   asleep

it is still morning   after all

•

eleven-headed kannon
female buddha that she is
her sleeve tilts
against her thigh

"to jump into
the stem of a lotus"

upright as forgiveness in her
hand mercy burnt into camphor

a monk found her double   & later
a warrior   helpless in the same
forest   who left the battle

1969/76

guided

she points
to a pine-tree
on the mountain

her gesture
repeats

old prints also
trace its branches

how they gather
the landscape

their makers
studied its line
& painted so

●

& the boy
in the print
points up

sakura no hana
to see what we got
everyone in april

o mi ni ikimasu
though she isn't
the procession

the branches
already fold over
her shoulders

from a passage in "the secret of the golden flower"

all things looked
upon as waxy

      this is delusion

all things step back
in the lap of emptiness

      this is centre

all things bring
grievances to

busy in the midst of
      business in the midst of
            practise in the midst of
ten thousand things

discarded hockey poem

cutting makes of
your skin a thread

they make of it
what they make of it

tall forms
or slender ones

flecked or brittle

making their way
back to the dressing room

make of them
what you make of them

the skin,   is the skin

•

they come of their own
without wings

to slide without
mirrors to bring them

to the surface of their moving
do they rise?

do they fall?
they are clouds behind a wall

breaking through like veins
nothing levels off

crawl under a fence into the bushes
there are thin leaves

sequins

moss garden
rock garden

●

butterfly dead
in the lane

orange & black
coalesce

the sparrows
cautious

in
tense

●

o may
you as well
xxxx tongue
tied to shore
like a stick

●

if the heart
is a bundle
of ends

move it,

for comfort
anything else

(unless one moves
there is no point

●

packet of lies
to stuff
the border of love

knocked on
they're hollow

sun or tree
they're inside

for sure
there's something
then sings
of unseen things

from the west side

(for way

the stream
coming on the ocean
is too cold
my feet are numb

the heron
  has one eye
    on you

late afternoon sun
pool of mercury

watch it

  •

watch it

a branch of evergreen
caught by two rocks
slippery over the stones

the heron is watching
  the jack of herons
    the corner of his eye

the branch is not seaweed
it floats again
straight for the sea   .

bring it back

this is my son
stone-in-hand

the stream pushes
through the opening

the branch nearly unstuck
the tail of it hooked
ready to go

bare legs your back
bent over the ledge
nothing to take
issue with

another stone?
throw it in

the heron?
the ocean

the ocean?
the heron

the heron?
is gone

sansei poem

one

it is a long line — so it is said
my grandfather & grandmother are primary

two photographs
miniatures
      'the bearer whose photograph
& specimen of signature appear hereon
has been duly registered in compliance
with the provisions of order-in-council
p.c. 117'
        there is my grandmother
on another surface

she — 4'11" & 130 lbs
he — 5'2½" & 127 lbs

photographs & signatures
with thumbprints

the neat letters of my grandfather
in english my grandmother's in kanji
in english her letters shake
she scratched one attempt

they are almost broken
she could barely close a circle
to form the o: for ooto
— 'large sound'

behind hardly noticeable
a piece of her husband
her face nearly turns away
they were naturalized

as for 'marks of identification'
— none for my grandfather
my grandmother had a
mole on her chin

two

there is
no battle

what you
turn into

this is
before me

(birds in the air
    of a branch
                which night
for the moment feeds

three

you came this way
once in a subway
(i waved)

dressed in a pin-stripe suit
with a chain suspended
from its vest pocket

i waved again you
stood drawn toward me
& missed the train

first one then
another crowd formed

now you stood diagonally
to the left
as they slid off
& i waved a third time

i was standing by the rail
beside the sign with the name
of the next stop
& was about to say
something again something
you might have heard

i stepped forward
to find the sign
between us

did your attention do this?
or did you intend
an old-fashioned stroll
through a museum of mirrors
on the far side of town?

i passed it on for you
could have been swallowed
in the tunnel with the others

i couldn't put together more
than a roundness & some lines

four

        at any time she was there
her face pressed like a flower
against the glass of the front door

             we hid behind
the curtains

        or when we expected her   on
the edge of the stair just inside the door

or the dark of the house did not satisfy
her & she circled around to the
back

    when this too failed   she broke off
& swung into the streets again mouthing
what she couldn't walk on

            they preceded her
incessantly

      & those times we met her
outside as we often did
nothing could stop her
from trailing us home

five

& to be among   there are
no   roots
there   ships wait
to be moved   and they
too cross   the pacific
once   we said
we say   the world lay
a mixture   the sun
the sea   our children
like marigolds   our boats
our nets   we
filled our houses   now
thin & brittle   the cold clings
now   the inland sea

six

it comes to one name
instead of another
or one place
more than another

is the air
dense with flies?

voices scatter like shadows
easily over a ridge

       down the path
       through the field
       to the streetcar
       into the city

which city?

       they swarmed they
could have been more
so they were nameless
the day shed its skin

seven

relocation — the least of
them waiting like statues

the orchard would be replaced
no semblances

photographs lost in a trunk
& later seen for sale

the sky is blue &
deep as it is wide

of course
of course

they would they say
pry the clouds loose
to float again

eight

there are eyes looking in
& eyes looking out

the eyes looking out
are deep & distant

they are only half-eyes
seeing a less proportionate way

they are eyes looking in
seeing what has come out

the eyes looking out for
the first time looking in

nine

it must have felt as if
a rock were wedged between
the inner & outer chambers

the others took it ahead to
inspect the curve of the river

you stayed behind on the slope
of the bank to scan once more
the bare uncertain wavering

they could have been birds
dancing the heat of wires
they could have been clothes

strung out
like names
no planes

ten

they will not so
neatly lie
down & be quieted

it was neatness
they were driven to

do they shake their skins
in cold air to remind
themselves of it?

the words froze
they did not dis-
appear behind them

     who comes here
with nothing but desire
as i do —

        another wind
       moves in disguise

look at their eyes
are they marbles
or cat's eyes?

the rustling of leaves

i drive down the street
& nothing pleases
no beauty to speak

empty playgrounds
grass so soggy
the feet like sponge

soak up the rain
that's been falling three days
& you say let it go at that

the rain renews all hollow
pain that can't be renewed
by a drive down the street

•

you drive the street
& nothing eases
no beauty speaks

in empty playgrounds
the grass so soggy
feet soak up the pain

rising now three days
& you say let it go at
that the rain renews

all hallow pain
that can't be renewed
by a drive down the street

●

trouble is
the i talks
& words walk
into the blue

that's you
in the shadows
snickering away

"with your
basket of words"

●

go down to the ground then
with the maple trees above you
the green laughter in the leaves
to turn the key & throw into gear

do whatever you do then
the opaque windows all covered
wipers stuck in place
your car encased in wet sap
the triumph of the trees again

●

winter's come on us
wet leaves, etc.
cover my overgrown lawn
dirt mounds
& potholes
with drain tiles, etc.

•

hand-me-downs, old shoes
on the lawn
covered by dry bits of grass

so there i've
begun an inventory
when the need's least

my hair drying
or dying in the sun
the back porch drenched in heat

all the way
over the line
of broken glass

where eyes
get lost in light

tiny pieces absorbing the lust
of graphic joy, the overjoyed scene
myself strutting — & faking out across
a blue lake, early autumn

vancouver — mt currie

the inside of head
wind blows my hat brim

never throw anything away
never keep anything

stop on a line
back up

there must be a way
to keep it all going

brain storm the hills

•

it could be
(in the space of) a second
(yes) it could be
(that) easily
in (that) space

you could drift
off (to sleep)
(on) the road
& the car
slide (through) the embankment
& roll
(into) the sea

•

"beaten at his
own game"

the wrought
words

rot on
his lips

pemberton liquor store

hot & sticky
cool interior

     5 natives
     3 whites
     & myself

natives against the counter
spaced out in a line
the scene's been going on
nobody looking at anybody

2 whites working the counter
lean over into an order form

another white hunched over
the other side
head to head to head

1 walks into an office
partitioned off &
circles puffing a cigarette

5 natives still as statues
"when do we get the business"
muttering sounds muffled
stray about the room

1 of 2 whites raises his head
walks around the counter
to the building's end
comes back with a gallon jug
of bc wine wrapped in a bag
& hands it over the head
of 1 old native first in line

his dimes nickels & pennies
as if the counter were a
checkerboard all lined up
dimes with dimes
nickels with nickels
& pennies with pennies
in a row the pennies first
then the nickels & finally the dimes

he stares down at them
changing 1 dime & 1 nickel
each with the other
& never disturbs the pattern

now he looks up
at the bottle over his head
& turns back for another one
kept within reach

as his coins disappear
first the dimes then the nickels
& finally the pennies
leaving him

   3 dimes
   1 nickel
   2 pennies

just words

in the midst of typing

& waylen who's now four
comes screaming into the study

ali's got a bird in her mouth
outside she's gone outside

the sentence in mid-air
? says something i don't catch

where are you going?
outside to bury the bird

it's dead then
no

then why are you burying it?

notebook entry on flight

to open *a dream of riches*
photo history of japanese
canadians 1877-1977

:   pass roger's watermelon
over the seat

>   on the way to ottawa
>   marie in front
>   michiko behind asleep
>   to the right koko roger
>   kuniko connie

>> behind 2 rows
>> back randy

18 months later
on the way
to the nation's capital

ba
ba

ba
sho

thou shouldst
be with us

some place

as a kid the ghost town
was some place
you came from
not *you* but anyone
with baggage & gifts

& the letters
everyone listening
the room suddenly circular

& always the ghost town
many many names
but always the *the*

so and so's cousin or aunt or brother
or daughter or second cousin by marriage
to the son of a grandfather

the whole web
of intricate family ties
spun off with no beginning or end
more than the matter of a theme

'you should see
them towns with nobody in them
the buildings fronted
like sets of an old movie
no one any longer wants to see
& all of them just there
you should see them for yourselves'

the slender voices
crowd into the narrow
margin of the page

the alternate sources of energy
are drying up

useless the words
that fall like snowflakes
over a stubbled plain

useless the operations
of the heart
abreast of time

useless the rooster that crows
the finite flowers
& the row of dead dreams
waiting to be covered
like birds of a feather

      i'm useless
with hammer & saw
& would rather hear
than see the ink dry

bulbs & briars
& forgetmenots do not
a full head make

•

blessed the tidy sums
blessed the trim lawns
blessed the loss of memory

     of a line
     that lights a page
     & is gone before
     the graphite
     spirit of
     bruised elbows

blessed the pockets
of penumbral air

•

a qua
train

aqua
train

device
& slice

from last
to aghast

the heart
sighs

not wise
to be apprised

in surprise
sunrise

•

"memory dies on the prairies"
i thought that up
when i was 12 & under
the railway bridge over
the assiniboine river

cool nights
between the ties
stars here & there

in the corners
the metal beams
meet to form
nests of pigeons

they've reproduced
over the river
in this space
where perspective
beckons below the brown
water moves as a street does

five takes for a poem on family

my grandmother dies
in the middle of the night
one day bent over
to pick something up
from the floor in the living room
of our old house on alexander street
in winnipeg
& she fell

a few days later
simply weakened & died
in the middle of the night
my father mother uncle
& i asked to stay up
to watch her die
on the bed
off the living room

her face her body
breathing heavily ever so often
until the middle of the night
she heaved
first softly
then louder & louder
the air blocked in a final vacuum
& the blood
the red drained from her face

•

my mother
works at the tannery
in the city
when the war ends

that day japan surrenders
my grandfather refuses
japan surrender?
never never never

my mother speechless at work
so they are defeated
what can she say
to that?

no one speaks
though she shrinks
into a smile

"yes father
the war is finally over"
& over & over & over

●

re-reading *the enemy*
that never was

the "evacuees" in manitoba
better off?

history tells such
beautiful lies

& if
& if

silly as putty
my 5 year old son
born in vancouver
makes a train
out of

barges in with it

charges out with it

zip zap zooooooom

•

"of song's destruction
the inert pauses"

first day
on the road
to okanagan falls

& elisse cried
all the way

screaming in time
to the muffled hum
of the engine

•

in fukuoka your photo
in kimono so vertical
unabashed & modest

& another alongside
the west coast trees
caught in the left
& right corners

on the veranda circled
by children a baby in arms
(perhaps my mother

others moving behind
my grandfather's casual
arm in the corner

it's after dinner &
someone with camera
visits & you in cotton sit
on a 4-legged chair

legs slightly apart
shoulder length hair
parted by a pin

born in manitoba?

(for gordon hirabayashi
who asked)

dropped before birth
i know it's the image
but i was dropped

like an apple?
certainly not like
an apple

like a rock? in
clouds of fine dust
on the prairies
those shapes
everyone stops
what they're doing

nothing dropped
when i was born
my certificate says
the winnipeg general

though not so simply told
what's meant by general

my mother in ste agathe
went off to the general

the nurses astonished
waited for the baby

to stare into the well's eye
for them a wishing well

drew from coolest mineral
black prairie well one
beginning for starts

as i was saying

crazy john who ran the neighbourhood
by catching you off guard

crazy john who snuck up behind
with his eyeballs rolling

crazy john who stayed
in the same grade
year after year
& never complained

who played hookey
& was never sought

who broke every rule
& was never chastised

crazy john who was the model citizen
of childhood haze in backyard lanes
his large jaw & brown hair
dusty in the sunlight

who never heard of ethnicity &
cultural pluralism & minority rights
who had no history

whose laughter
swelled in his neck
& came rushing out of his mouth

6 feet tall
when he was 12?

hard to say
how to tell

ok falls

night sound

rock & roll on the beach
the far away sound
of speakers trapped
by lake air

the sound of air conditioners
like a chorus of dying saints

"fast rising"
"effet rapide"

●

sequences occur
in diurnal fits
of like frenzy

a pair of white butterflies
wrestle in mid-flight
they dally

the beat of the hose
shutter speed
1/250

●

the registered guests
are in slender supply
by the chlorinated pool

turquoise   (sun reflected
plastic skin   the instant
fast as it goes   lingers
(amber in places   mountains

however that goes
in the saying it
begets platitude
served on dishes
left last year

•

those easy exits
left of escape

those near the dark
holes of suspense

across the chasm
of forgetfulness

you never step into
the same words twice

or once as the sign says
nestled in oliver's orchard
face to the road

"heaven & earth shall pass
away (but) my words
shall not pass"

•

sanctuary's the refuse
mind makes many
such places enchanted
phosphorescent time

what lies told
them to hold

o disrespectful sparrow
that you should be so common
& not the iris of butterflies
& not the muse of birds

(the body forked & curved
lies under the apple tree

•

no   sanctuary's not
thing nor refuge
the a(b)jective
to re(e)fer
or be(e)

brand x
deludes us

brand x
covers us

with nothing
brand x

cancels
period

i
city

•

wind at my back so
late summer leaves settle
the rust in my brains

•

o god as i've been
here in the yard
lost in thoth

it's filled with birds
sleek starlings
sparrows & robins
the tribes linger
in sprinkler made space

the sun's day
the moon's day

so sure the common porpoise
lost purpose long ago

voices like trunks of trees
dumb to motion though

fluttering tips
of sweet talking jargon

i've been now

for months in undated season
between the great pillars
of a walking dream

& the sea set for closure
in dire straits
seeks a lover's dwelling

death dives down
& regales the rushed heart

no biography or
the remembering splayed

i was to figure
what came first

call it naivete
or the dwindling of active verbs

the tenses & the erotic interplay
of bone with siphoned air

bare assed
& dray bleached

terminal heartaches
like thyme time

cast out of any topography
the line disengages

where one begins
innumerable non-descriptive
unquotable pockets of words

failed tanka

in the personal
ashes of our discontent

dumpheap clues lit up

the spectacle of kind red
flares & the tongue lashes out

flat poem

the body spins & spuns
on the eve of all days

hungers & wastes away
little remains   a dash

across the street

      rain
      clouds

      wet
      pavement

the dead grass & mud
feet to the garbage
is this all?

the pail stolen & what's left
strewn across the back lane

beginning middle end

says the whole order
no no no no no no

the decay of truth
no no no no no no

the whole truth
& nothing but the
no no no no no no

the thin line between
signs on the highway pointing

turn turn turn
like the old song said

in the dream of beginnings
in the time of birds
bye bye blackbird

why don't you sit right down
& write someone a letter

& make believe it came
from you?

a pure language doesn't exist
scarred verbs are lost nouns

prepositions become
propositions become
hardened into factum

i yoked & a blackbird
perched on the street sign

looking in my window
as i sat writing this
watching a blackbird

hey there
you with the stars
in your eyes

has shifted
& time is a stone
sitting on the lawn

& turning to stone
is progress
is the slow boat to china

light poem

the bike she rides
oval face in wind

laughter that her body
should so move

that the motor action
of her legs should carry her
across the parking lot

light broke from
the shadowy woods
where the lone eagle
perched on the pine

& she goes round & round
sky streaked with cloud lines

twinge of guilt
that the morning is spent
spent mind you

sitting on the curb
with the words
there in space

the bike is meta
physical

ephemera
eph   em   'er

ra
spoke glint

lumen de lumine

lilac enfolds
debris walls

studded earth
bush whacked

per capita
sea wash

round rhythm
defused puddles

past fields
light trails

dusk settlers
& supermarkets

seeds blunder
sky blue

high stubble
wind streams

rain drain
age seeps

that hath
no place

lace
ace

charles olson says

in the end   when all
the estrangement is over
when the familiar

is known   who isn't up
against the face of god
like a wall

or a mirror where the shadow
or the cut-out shape
or the light is the reflection

or the light
or the figure of himself
in species?

reality is unfinished business
or there would be no extent
and the time

that man knows
comes to know
when he stares

is what history
enables him to confirm
that the extent is a limit

history is the confidence
of limit as man is caught

on the assumption
and power of change
(fr *a special view of history*)

found

honest wes
i don't know
where to start

things happen
so fast
i'm in a daze

& nothing affects
much now
i mean everything

no sadness
when friends
disappear overnight

to camp or
somewhere in the interior
no farewells

no promise of meetings
or correspondence
we just disperse

(in a letter march 12/42
from muriel kitagawa
to her brother wes

two powell st festival haiku

nisei blues

"hey i've got time to burn"
leaves around us on the grass —
at last, oh at least!

festival time

internment photos
hanging on wobbly tent walls —
gusts of the camp snow

a redress note

(on the way to toronto, march 1)

. . . an immersion process, s and the kids so in touch with
its specificity. the party at the house sat evening, with my
mother from wpg, was the culmination of a long
unravelling, one knot after another — filled daily with
apprehension but on the edge of a history that brings the
world (mundus) into a precious alignment. never thought
it possible in my generation to witness, not just witness
but be involved in the phenomenal shifting going on
within this internal space of our lives as jcs.

45 people there, variation in age from e, 5, to 80. and w,
now 12, as word in action, moving thru the fluid
conversation, so "articulate" in the social dynamics —
clearing dishes, serving drinks, keeping everyone going.
in his element, & e too, who is a dream to us, her heart
so insistent.

such moments of clarity in a contemporary milieu with its
sickening social model emptied of spirit, the patterned
responses. we seem blessed, in this (meta) transiency,
with access to the finitude of our lives, in the fragility of
potential cessation each second.

memo for joy kogawa

elation &
deflation

(the rhythm

heave &
pull

(the disaster

stretch of
my kids' arms

winsome figures
win some thought

(the outward

on the road
the figures dance

(they dance

7:53 am

redress

accidental meeting

(for tom shoyama

aboard jet
lag time

where the
past takes off

& the present
begins

disguised event
this meeting

turns in a date
faces at the window

only accidental
they say

over ottawa
redress on my mind

& you
off to quebec city

to heal
the economy

though i say
the economy of words

these days
history speaks

& we
listen

& we ride
these airwaves

between time?
i think not

daily the news
grows thick

i could go
on talking

but for
landing time

as history
says

see you later
later

in flight notes

clear now the government set up that meeting with their "officials" DB, OK, and AS to define the NAJC's position and dilute public support. as OK sd at the jan 12 meeting the government never ever intended to negotiate. they've long dealt with us via double standards, so it comes easily for them. minister jm in private bullies us and uses intimidation tactics . . . .

jcs have nothing other than the rightness of the cause, their strength, but their weakness is awe before the power of authority. once the government threatens to discredit them they tend to buckle and give in to their fears that continued challenge will bring retaliation and censure from the white community, forgetting that the struggle for justice involves risk and the need to maintain the inner perspective against the external pressure to compromise.

we can't compromise the community's right to appeal for real compensation for the wholesale obliteration of lives and livelihood, the degradation and the humiliation — last evening at a house meeting — the barbarism of confinement in the livestock stalls at hastings park, the barbarism of confinement in chicken shacks on the prairie sugar beet fields. lost dreams, and the searing sense of betrayal, held in, but present in the stories.

(from a notebook, 27 jan 85, on the way to ottawa)

•

bod
body
bag
bod
bo
bought

sought
seek
eek
beak

sentenced
by story

mirrored
by forehead

foresight
by freight

facts take
bending willows
image cloak

one says
surely the roar
winds down to the sea

history
takes time

one gets
wary?

weary from talk
brain rumble
seat wheat

fields

kome's story

(for auntie nagasaki

it's the same story
told again & again

the modulations
& the machinations

the maudlin
& the dream

schemes & data
a million documents

& a single story
kome's

she said she
moved into her house

her dream house
on december 6th

fell into a deep sleep
stirred the dream

to wake
to war

& the splitting apart
her son

sent off to petawawa
barbed wire

her husband
to tête jaune

herself to
greenwood

green
wood?

ghost
town?

new names
her memory

& the train
(later

to montreal
"the commission

said there'd
be jobs there"

5 days
4 nights

sitting & sleeping
in the coach

dreaming of
the coast

the french tongue
the english tongue

words
& words

o
canada

brief poem

this is
a true story

i was sitting
in a plane

air canada
flight to toronto

minding my business
reading the redress brief

half way to ottawa
to check the footnotes

make sure we weren't
talking through our hats

as they say
& i was working

furiously
against time

as i usually do
& next to me

he was already asking me
what the jc community was up to

so i explained
the changing sphere

of perceptions
saying most of the things

i say in
like circumstances

& he was agreeing
(between talk of

landscape
ocean & horizon

the continent between
east & west

& i was rehearsing
the landscape

of facts
we were unearthing

he said
he'd be watching

out for news
& he said

his name
was ian mackenzie•

• liberal mp for vancouver centre, notorious for his
antagonism toward jcs, and as pm mackenzie king's adviser,
the most influential politician in the decision to mass uproot
them from the west coast. it was he who declared in his
nomination speech, 18 sept 1944, "let our slogan be for
british columbia: 'no japs from the rockies to the seas'."

victim's song

yr honour i come
of humble origins
born in a remote
corner of yr kingdom

the blank spaces of
my childhood filled
with spotted marigolds

at yr height with
perspective on yr side
like the old masters
who glorified the landscape
& made words shine
as the sun's rays

do did done on me
& my kinfolk who
meandered in yr realm

spots on the horizon
grey blue lines
mountains in yr mind

scattered ranges
where waves peak
& break

in my village
stories are
sent by telepathy

sad to say this
has rendered us
bereft of speech

forgive me for approaching
but these late days

i am seduced as a factor
in yr economies of scale

o yr honour
as the riddles dwindle
& ashen faces of subjects
sigh into a sheen

listen as my
electronic bones
explode in splendour

higher learning

(from a letter to the
consul general of spain
from the office of the
canadian secretary of state
12 july 1943)

1. the living & working
   habits of occidentals are
   so different from those

   of the japanese that tenants
   who are at once permanent &
   satisfactory cannot be secured.

2. an untenanted farm obviously
   must soon be ruined.

3. under these circumstances
   the only policy
   which would preserve

   & protect the investments
   of the japanese owner is
   to liquidate the property.

4. most of the japanese
   have refused to recognize
   the wisdom of this step but

   being confident that it
   is in the best interests
   of the property owners

   the government proposes
   to follow it.

press re lease

(in response to an editorial•

to ottawa   middle sea(t
muddle of notes   scattered the
encapsulated basement   room
w)here the news filters   popping corn

the kids shower   on the phone
working out strategy   say the
chronology of events   time pressure
words tighten   the frame
as the g&m editor says   "perspective
please"   the analogy disturbs
synchronic & accident   incidence
hey   speech pressure   quotes in
the paper   out of   perspective
flat objects   flung across
the room   dispersed
become   a locality

• from *the globe & mail*, 26 jan 85: ". . . when mr. m____
heard that the cabinet might unilaterally approve a sum
(said to be $6-million), he reacted this way: 'they're saying,
"you've got three weeks to agree to this." it's like, "you've got
24 hours to pack your bags and leave the coast. we're doing
it for your own good." '

"perspective, please. what is in dispute is the nature and
amount of redress, not the principle. while multiculturalism
minister jack murta's talk of a 'memorialization' may fall
short of what is needed, the government has acknowledged
the injustice of the internment, a position which is light-
years from 1941 and, indeed, from 1984, when former
prime minister pierre trudeau rejected the notion even of
an apology.

"mr. m____ wants the government to negotiate further;
fair enough. but to draw a parallel between the disputed
details of this settlement and the actions of the wartime
government is absurd."

planetary frame
work pressure to say
the analogy holds

weight?

water seeks its own
in the welter of events
doubts hard as stone

my parents'
"we had 24 hours
to pack & leave"

believe me
one day

a lifetime
of repetitions
of one & one & one

the popcorn
fills the pot

•

one moves   dimension to signal
nodes of energy   knots in flow
the i   a cross   the distances

story tells
"perspective please"

hey don't talk
in image

say i
mage

•

one's story   would be silent
the body   accomplishes only
so much noise   but ah

"when i have fears
that i may cease
to be"

as the poet   would have us say
distortions tell   i am bound
& unravelling   the way to ottawa
's paved with stones

made the words
measure the body's spillage

"the language is missing them
& they die incommunicado"

as the poet
would have us
say cell talk

"you've got 24 hours   to get out"
"perspective please"   he says "light years"
from 1941

the popcorn is flying
talking strategy
the phone line
crosses distance

the kids run
from the shower
scoop it up

for the rumour mill
i must check out

the etymology
of the word

in flight

the aspiration to be
non-semantic

eg i was asked
just now —

interruption of baggage
stowed under the seat

could i accommodate
the baby behind me
& the elderly lady?

her dark eyes
in foreign continent

across the aisle?
the passageway?

who sidles over
into centre space

i'd give three to one
if she'd catch my drift

•

so no words
for existence

so what else
is new

we championed
its advent —

(god why are my
lines disappearing
into disfiguration?

76

if you'd be alive
to declare love

in faith that time
is enough

•

why choose
to be in

form is not enough
to satisfy desire

i de-
sire you

s' ire in sacrifice for
the sake of the children

the i in subzero
is also claritas

creek i swam as a child
cold as the body
in the crevices

•

i said it's so long 2
more hours to vancouver
& she said it's less than 5

honestly
why prolong history?

fortunes told
fortunes lost

"throw momma from the train"
on the video

the rain mother i row
no poet
am i

to sign my
life away

•

binding the skin to word
that's the rub

kid's saying
the age is not ripe
for fruition

history —
the abstract
i love

that's everywhere
in disrepute

in polite circles
the verb is obsolete

the human is
only promise

so i dedicate
this absence

●

lost in my
own awareness

a child crying
my own (in memory)
air rushing by

we could be
other so fast

history is we

(partially stolen title

signing waivers
o legal jargon

choice for lunch
steak or fish

earth or sea
two components

of settlement
belief in elements

breaks the law
of disfigurement

cool tongues caress
my lover's lips

geo
graphic

of blood lines
by the light

of silver
moon scan

screen dream
of filial ties

unwinding highway
rock cliffs

promontories
of nerves

endings
& them

•

i can't believe
belief leaf

of the old tree
honey in the home

bee hive
i can't

believe it's
been one

year (ear
did'ya say

one ear
tuned to ash

since last
note entrance

on board these
waves of air

scared
scar/red

•

redolence aspires
a spire with beam
of light   (dispersed they have

all gone the way of particles
motes across the mountain range

the intelligence?   only smoke
no fire in the heart's
body to find one's own

definitions & leery hopes
to catch the rhyme
climb the incline

on track
holy smoke
the iron will

the backslide down
(drowned in the
daily the daily

grows daily
grows daily

the daily
daily

legislate against change
permanence & monument
against transition of power

the personal & local
become will of the wisp

the forge of event
filed in closed brackets

isolated insignias mellow
weather blather incorporated

seed implanted sorrow
this motion abused inchoate

•

sent by
sense by
scent by

the way how d'you
get to the sea

which entrance gave
exit to wavering?

i dog along
the boardwalk by
the logical beaches

sand dunes
done in

•

dew on the brow
the transient
bereft of speech

sign of the times
history of more words
than you can carry

beyond the corridor
i blend into the past

clear the web
of brain waves

•

fear of trust
& the tongue slides
over the dial

stations of the way
memorabilia to tuck away
where the line gets drawn

single purpose?

the whirlwind tour
the horizon looks
clear up here —

diffidence in the doorway
syllables in the drainage

fine night to be
standing in rain mist

crowds on yonge street
willing over celluloid

instant of what
am i saying
seeing etc etc

re
cognition

& the talk turns on
group vs individual

the cross of burden
i heard said

we is i
in the vocab
we is one

excuse me
i'm patient

the sky again
(blue) sky

& the inching
back home

way of the locus

(for george bowering

so deeply engrossed
in the metaphysics

of life in the bus
i was so unnaturally

abstracted thinking
the general is the case

in ottawa
no kidding

& she was gesturing
toward her forehead

to pick away dead skin
just as i do too

but her hand moved
zen fashion down

she looked for frag
ments in fingernails

& i figured you'd see
if any one poet would

tho i confess to being just
a victim of circumstance

22 sept 88

(for bpnichol
who died 25 sept 88

settle meant?

"me ant"
a state meant

mean mea me
only words

some one sd
words'll only

get us there
to here ere er

re dress
decked out

h eir
   air
   err

the future (w)ring
the present (w)ro(ugh)t
the past (w)rung

•

"i know . . . i speak for
members on all sides

of the house today
in offering to jcs the

formal and sincere apology
of this parliament for those

past injustices against them"
(the pm, hansard, hc)

Glossary

obaa-chan gakko iko	"Grandma, I'm going to school."
obaasan	grandmother
sansei	third generation Japanese Canadian
nisei	second generation Canadian-born Japanese Canadian
nihonjin	Japanese people
daikon	a radish
gobo	a root
kannon	Japanese goddess of mercy
sakura no hana	cherry blossoms
o mi ni ikimasu	"goes to see"
Secret of the Golden Flower	*Secret of the Golden Flower: A Chinese Book of Life.* C.G. Jung. Trans. Richard Wilhelm. Harcourt Brace Jovanovich, 1970.
ooto	"large sound" but also a family name
Pemberton	a town in B.C., near the Mt. Currie native reserve
"ba sho"	Basho, the Japanese poet
The Enemy That Never Was	*The Enemy That Never Was.* Ken Adachi. Toronto: McClelland & Stewart, 1979. A history of Japanese Canadians.
Fukuoka	a city in Japan, on the island of Kyushu
ok falls	Okanagan Falls, a B.C. town
Oliver	a B.C. town
tanka	Japanese poetic form
lumen de lumine	"light of light"; title of a work by Thomas Vaughan
haiku	Japanese poetic form

NAJC	National Association of Japanese Canadians
Petawawa	site of a prisoner of war camp in Ontario during the second world war
tête jaune	Yellowhead, in B.C.
commission	The B.C. Security Commission, in charge of the mass uprooting of Japanese Canadians
redress brief	*Democracy Betrayed*, submitted to the government on November 21, 1984
"when I have fears"	from Keats' "Sonnet vii"
"the language is missing them"	from William Carlos Williams' *Paterson*
"me ant"	from bpNichol's *gifts*

Photo: Cassandra Kobayashi

Roy Miki grew up in Ste. Agathe and Winnipeg, after federal authorities forcibly uprooted his parents from their home in British Columbia. He later moved back to B.C. where he now teaches Canadian and American literature at Simon Fraser University. He has been a central figure in the redress movement which seeks compensation for the treatment of Japanese Canadians during and after the Second World War at the hands of the federal government.

Roy Miki has given numerous lectures and seminars and published many articles on the history of Japanese Canadians. His scholarship includes a critical study and compilation of the works of Muriel Kitagawa entitled *This Is My Own: Letters to Wes & Other Writings on Japanese Canadians, 1941-1948*. Roy Miki is the editor of *West Coast Line* and has edited several critical texts, including *Tracing the Paths*, essays on bpNichol, and *A Record of Writing*, a bibliography of George Bowering.